Visiting the
POLICE STATION

Joan Chapman

The Rosen Publishing Group, Inc.
New York

Police officers report to the police station every day before their workday starts.

Inside the police station you will see a police officer sitting behind a desk.

Police officers come to work and meet with their **captain.** The captain tells the officers what their **duties** will be for the day.

Police officers can have different kinds of jobs. **Patrol officers** walk or drive through **neighborhoods** to help people follow **laws**.

Many officers drive patrol cars.
Officers turn on the **siren** and
lights when they want drivers to
pull over.

This police officer works with a police dog to find drugs. A police dog is trained to smell drugs even when they are hidden.

You can call **911** for help when someone is sick or hurt. The person who answers will call the police station.

A person at the police station
will call the patrol officer on his
or her car radio. Then the patrol
officer can come to help you.

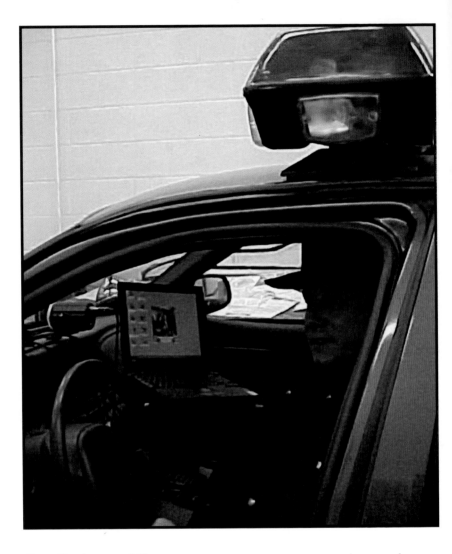

Police officers use computers in their cars or at the station. They use them to find out facts when someone breaks a law.

Police officers work hard to make sure everyone follows the laws. Police officers help us stay safe.

Glossary

captain A police officer who is the leader of the group.

duty Work that someone must do at his or her job.

law A rule for all people.

neighborhood The streets and houses around where you live.

911 A phone number that is called to get help quickly.

patrol officer A person who walks or drives through places to help keep people safe.

siren Something on a police car that makes a loud sound.